Memorize this Book

by Philip Stein

Memorize this Book

by Philip Stein

A Smart Smiles Company LLC Book

Introduction

In *Memorize this Book,* you will find a variety of selections from history's finest poetry, philosophy, music lyrics, and literature. They were chosen for their eternal beauty and relevance. Some are written in a somewhat antiquated style of English, but should nevertheless be easily understandable to readers. Perhaps the primary consideration in our selection process is that we deem them worthy of the time and effort that will be required to commit them to memory, and we know that you will never regret this effort. It will require a regular ongoing commitment for an extended period of time, ranging in most cases from months to years. The benefits and rewards of such an undertaking are certainly worth it, but make no mistake – this will be a challenging endeavor.

However, once you have achieved your goal of committing the entire book to memory, or have achieved intermediate goals of memorizing individual selections from the book, you will feel empowered, richer, and "smarter." Imagine the feeling of having some of the greatest phrases and thoughts ever conceived available in your mind and on the "tip of your tongue," during periods of challenge and times of joy, allowing you to reflect on such moments from the perspective of these great historical figures.

There are a variety of memory techniques that have been developed over thousands of years, collectively known as "The Arts of Memory." These include the "Mnemonic Link System," a variation called "Memory Palace," or more traditionally, the "Method of Loci," in which you picture a place or building very familiar to you and then create a story incorporating the material you are memorizing in combination with that place. For instance, if a poem starts off with the mention of birds, you would start your imagined story in your familiar place, with birds flying around a particular room. If "blue sky" is mentioned soon after, you would perhaps continue the story with the birds flying around a skylight open to the blue sky, and so on. Some who utilize this technique suggest that the more absurd the story, the more memorable...perhaps, then, those birds should go crashing into the skylight trying to escape to the "blue sky."

The technique we recommend for maximum mental benefit and satisfaction is sometimes referred to as the "Rote Learning" method, which involves repetitive reading, then reading aloud, then writing or typing the material while reading it aloud. Each of these steps is done multiple times until the particular piece is committed to memory. Any of the steps may be skipped, though the combination of all steps is generally believed to be most effective.

It is always easier to memorize when one feels an emotional connection to the material. We are sure you will find the beauty and inspiration found in the material we have chosen to be a great advantage in this regard. You will simply want to claim all this wonderful material "for your own."

Perhaps many of you are purchasing this book based on the research that has been done in the field of cognitive function, especially regarding how mental exercise - including memorization - can provide ongoing benefits to all of us, and particularly to the elderly who may be facing some degree of cognitive decline. Studies show that mental exercise can help prevent or delay such decline, with some studies even showing that it can help improve cognitive function in those already diagnosed with Alzheimer's disease. Just as one should do physical exercise to maintain the body's fitness, it is becoming more widely understood that one should also do mental exercise to maintain, and even improve, the function of the mind. We wish you luck, and we know you will consider it time well spent in a world where we are so busy with many less worthwhile endeavors.

The following "prompt" list will assist you in recalling the order of material once you have committed a substantial amount of the book to memory. This will prevent you from having to flip through the book to remember the order of the selections.

Content/Prompt list

Shall I compare thee to a summers day

Sonnet 18
William Shakespeare

Shall I compare thee to a summer's day?
Thou art more lovely and more temperate.
Rough winds do shake the darling buds of May,
And summer's lease hath all too short a date.
Sometime too hot the eye of heaven shines,
And often is his gold complexion dimmed;
And every fair from fair sometime declines,
By chance, or nature's changing course untrimmed.
But thy eternal summer shall not fade
Nor lose possession of that fair thou ow'st;
Nor shall death brag thou wand'rest in his shade,
When in eternal lines to time thou grow'st,
So long as men can breathe or eyes can see,
So long lives this, and this gives life to thee.

Daffodils

William Wordsworth

I wandered lonely as a cloud
That floats on high o'er vales and hills,
When all at once I saw a crowd,
A host, of golden daffodils;
Beside the lake, beneath the trees,
Fluttering and dancing in the breeze.

Continuous as the stars that shine
And twinkle on the milky way,
They stretched in never-ending line
Along the margin of a bay:
Ten thousand saw I at a glance,
Tossing their heads in sprightly dance.

The waves beside them danced, but they
Out-did the sparkling leaves in glee;
A poet could not be but gay,
In such a jocund company!
I gazed—and gazed—but little thought
What wealth the show to me had brought:

For oft, when on my couch I lie
In vacant or in pensive mood,
They flash upon that inward eye
Which is the bliss of solitude;
And then my heart with pleasure fills,
And dances with the daffodils.

Invictus

William Ernest Henley

Out of the night that covers me,
Black as the pit from pole to pole,
I thank whatever gods may be
For my unconquerable soul.

In the fell clutch of circumstance
I have not winced nor cried aloud.
Under the bludgeonings of chance
My head is bloody, but unbowed.

Beyond this place of wrath and tears
Looms but the Horror of the shade,
And yet the menace of the years
Finds and shall find me unafraid.

It matters not how strait the gate,
How charged with punishments the scroll,
I am the master of my fate:
I am the captain of my soul.

Romeo and Juliet

William Shakespeare

But soft! What light through yonder window breaks?
It is the East, and Juliet is the sun!
Arise, fair sun, and kill the envious moon,
Who is already sick and pale with grief
That thou her maid art far more fair than she.
Be not her maid, since she is envious.
Her vestal livery is but sick and green,
And none but fools do wear it. Cast it off.
It is my lady; O, it is my love!
O that she knew she were!
She speaks, yet she says nothing. What of that?
Her eye discourses; I will answer it.
I am too bold; 'tis not to me she speaks.
Two of the fairest stars in all the heaven,
Having some business, do entreat her eyes
To twinkle in their spheres till they return.
What if her eyes were there, they in her head?
The brightness of her cheeks would shame those stars
As daylight doth a lamp; her eyes in heaven
Would through the airy region stream so bright
That birds would sing and think it were not night.
See how she leans her cheek upon her hand!
O that I were a glove upon that hand,

That I might touch that cheek!

The Gettysburg Address

Abraham Lincoln

Four score and seven years ago our fathers brought forth on this continent, a new nation, conceived in Liberty, and dedicated to the proposition that all men are created equal.

Now we are engaged in a great civil war, testing whether that nation, or any nation so conceived and so dedicated, can long endure. We are met on a great battle-field of that war. We have come to dedicate a portion of that field, as a final resting place for those who here gave their lives that that nation might live. It is altogether fitting and proper that we should do this.

But, in a larger sense, we can not dedicate -- we can not consecrate -- we can not hallow -- this ground. The brave men, living and dead, who struggled here, have consecrated it, far above our poor power to add or detract. The world will little note, nor long remember what we say here, but it can never forget what they did here. It is for us the living, rather, to be dedicated here to the unfinished work which they who fought here have thus far so nobly advanced. It is rather for us to be here dedicated to the great task remaining before us -- that from these honored dead we take increased devotion to that cause for which they gave the last full measure of devotion -- that we here highly resolve that these dead shall not have died in vain -- that this nation, under God, shall have a new birth of freedom -- and that government of the people, by the people, for the people, shall not perish from the earth.

As You Like It

William Shakespeare

All the world's a stage,
And all the men and women merely players:
They have their exits and their entrances;
And one man in his time plays many parts,
His acts being seven ages. As, first the infant,
Mewling and puking in the nurse's arms.
And then the whining school-boy, with his satchel
And shining morning face, creeping like snail
Unwillingly to school. And then the lover,
Sighing like furnace, with a woeful ballad
Made to his mistress' eyebrow. Then a soldier,
Full of strange oaths and bearded like the pard,
Jealous in honour, sudden and quick in quarrel,
Seeking the bubble reputation
Even in the cannon's mouth. And then the justice,
In fair round belly with good capon lined,
With eyes severe and beard of formal cut,
Full of wise saws and modern instances;
And so he plays his part. The sixth age shifts
Into the lean and slipper'd pantaloon,
With spectacles on nose and pouch on side,
His youthful hose, well saved, a world too wide
For his shrunk shank; and his big manly voice,
Turning again toward childish treble, pipes
And whistles in his sound. Last scene of all,
That ends this strange eventful history,
Is second childishness and mere oblivion,
Sans teeth, sans eyes, sans taste, sans everything.

A Tale of Two Cities

Charles Dickens

It was the best of times,
it was the worst of times,
it was the age of wisdom,
it was the age of foolishness,
it was the epoch of belief,
it was the epoch of incredulity,
it was the season of Light,
it was the season of Darkness,
it was the spring of hope,
it was the winter of despair,
we had everything before us,
we had nothing before us,
we were all going direct to Heaven,
we were all going direct the other way--
in short, the period was so far like the present period,
that some of
its noisiest authorities insisted on its being received,
for good or for
evil, in the superlative degree of comparison only.

Preamble to the Declaration of Independence of the United States

Thomas Jefferson et al.

When in the Course of human events it becomes necessary for one people to dissolve the political bands which have connected them with another and to assume among the powers of the earth, the separate and equal station to which the Laws of Nature and of Nature's God entitle them, a decent respect to the opinions of mankind requires that they should declare the causes which impel them to the separation

We hold these truths to be self-evident, that all men are created equal, that they are endowed by their Creator with certain unalienable Rights, that among these are Life, Liberty and the pursuit of Happiness. — That to secure these rights, Governments are instituted among Men, deriving their just powers from the consent of the governed, — That whenever any Form of Government becomes destructive of these ends, it is the Right of the People to alter or to abolish it, and to institute new Government, laying its foundation on such principles and organizing its powers in such form, as to them shall seem most likely to effect their Safety and Happiness. Prudence, indeed, will dictate that Governments long established should not be changed for light and transient causes; and accordingly all experience hath shewn that mankind are more disposed to suffer, while evils are sufferable than to right themselves by abolishing the forms to which they are accustomed. But when a long train of abuses and usurpations, pursuing invariably the same Object evinces a design to reduce them under absolute Despotism, it is their right, it is their duty, to throw off such Government, and to provide new Guards for their future security.

For Whom the Bell Tolls

John Donne

No man is an island,
Entire of itself.
Each is a piece of the continent,
A part of the main.
If a clod be washed away by the sea,
Europe is the less.
As well as if a promontory were.
As well as if a manor of thine own
Or of thine friend's were.
Each man's death diminishes me,
For I am involved in mankind.
Therefore, send not to know
For whom the bell tolls,
It tolls for thee.

The Merchant of Venice

William Shakespeare

All that glitters is not gold;
Often have you heard that told:
Many a man his life hath sold
But my outside to behold:
Gilded tombs do worms enfold.
Had you been as wise as bold,
Young in limbs, in judgement old
Your answer had not been inscroll'd
Fare you well, your suit is cold.

Moby Dick

Herman Melville

Call me Ishmael. Some years ago--never mind how long precisely--having little or no money in my purse, and nothing particular to interest me on shore, I thought I would sail about a little and see the watery part of the world. It is a way I have of driving off the spleen and regulating the circulation. Whenever I find myself growing grim about the mouth; whenever it is a damp, drizzly November in my soul; whenever I find myself involuntarily pausing before coffin warehouses, and bringing up the rear of every funeral I meet; and especially whenever my hypos get such an upper hand of me, that it requires a strong moral principle to prevent me from deliberately stepping into the street, and methodically knocking people's hats off--then, I account it high time to get to sea as soon as I can. This is my substitute for pistol and ball. With a philosophical flourish Cato throws himself upon his sword; I quietly take to the ship. There is nothing surprising in this. If they but knew it, almost all men in their degree, some time or other, cherish very nearly the same feelings towards the ocean with me.

The Great Gatsby

F. Scott Fitzgerald

In my younger and more vulnerable years my father gave me some advice that I've been turning over in my mind ever since.

"Whenever you feel like criticizing any one," he told me, "just remember that all the people in this world haven't had the advantages that you've had."

He didn't say any more, but we've always been unusually communicative in a reserved way, and I understood that he meant a great deal more than that. In consequence, I'm inclined to reserve all judgments, a habit that has opened up many curious natures to me and also made me the victim of not a few veteran bores. The abnormal mind is quick to detect and attach itself to this quality when it appears in a normal person, and so it came about that in college I was unjustly accused of being a politician, because I was privy to the secret griefs of wild, unknown men. Most of the confidences were unsought — frequently I have feigned sleep, preoccupation, or a hostile levity when I realized by some unmistakable sign that an intimate revelation was quivering on the horizon; for the intimate revelations of young men, or at least the terms in which they express them, are usually plagiaristic and marred by obvious suppressions. Reserving judgments is a matter of infinite hope. I am still a little afraid of missing something if I forget that, as my father snobbishly suggested, and

I snobbishly repeat, a sense of the fundamental decencies is parceled out unequally at birth.

If

Rudyard Kipling

If you can keep your head when all about you
Are losing theirs and blaming it on you,
If you can trust yourself when all men doubt you,
But make allowance for their doubting too;
If you can wait and not be tired by waiting,
Or being lied about, don't deal in lies,
Or being hated, don't give way to hating,
And yet don't look too good, nor talk too wise:

If you can dream - and not make dreams your master,
If you can think - and not make thoughts your aim;
If you can meet with Triumph and Disaster
And treat those two impostors just the same;
If you can bear to hear the truth you've spoken
Twisted by knaves to make a trap for fools,
Or watch the things you gave your life to, broken,
And stoop and build 'em up with worn-out tools:
If you can make one heap of all your winnings
And risk it all on one turn of pitch-and-toss,
And lose, and start again at your beginnings
And never breath a word about your loss;
If you can force your heart and nerve and sinew
To serve your turn long after they are gone,
And so hold on when there is nothing in you
Except the Will which says to them: "Hold on!"

If you can talk with crowds and keep your virtue,
Or walk with kings - nor lose the common touch,
If neither foes nor loving friends can hurt you,

If all men count with you, but none too much;
If you can fill the unforgiving minute
With sixty seconds' worth of distance run,
Yours is the Earth and everything that's in it,
And - which is more - you'll be a Man, my son!

Lord of the Rings- The Fellowship of the Rings

J.R.R. Tolkien

All that is gold does not glitter;
not all those who wander are lost.
The old that is strong does not wither;
deep roots are not reached by the frost.
From the ashes a fire shall be woken;
a light from the shadows shall spring;
Renewed shall be the blade that was broken,
and crownless again shall be the King.

The Merchant of Venice

William Shakespeare

The quality of mercy is not strained.
It droppeth as the gentle rain from heaven
Upon the place beneath. It is twice blest:
It blesseth him that gives and him that takes.
Tis mightiest in the mightiest; it becomes
The throned monarch better than his crown.
His scepter shows the force of temporal power,
The attribute to awe and majesty,
Wherein doth sit the dread and fear of kings.
But mercy is above this sceptered sway;
It is enthroned in the hearts of kings;
It is an attribute of God himself;
And earthly power doth then show like God's
When mercy seasons justice.

Remembrance of Things Past

Marcel Proust

"There is no man," he began, "however wise, who has
not at some period of his youth said things, or lived
in a way the consciousness of which is so unpleasant
to him in later life that he would gladly, if he could,
expunge it from his memory. And yet he ought not
entirely to regret it, because he cannot be certain
that he has indeed become a wise man—so far as
it is possible for any of us to be wise—unless he
has passed through all the fatuous or unwholesome
incarnations by which that ultimate stage must be
preceded. I know that there are young fellows, the
sons and grandsons of famous men, whose masters
have instilled into them nobility of mind and moral
refinement in their schooldays. They have, perhaps,
when they look back upon their past lives, nothing
to retract; they can, if they choose, publish a signed
account of everything they have ever said or done;
but they are poor creatures, feeble descendants of
doctrinaires, and their wisdom is negative and sterile.
We are not provided with wisdom, we must discover
it for ourselves, after a journey through the wilderness
which no one else can take for us, an effort which no
one can spare us, for our wisdom is the point of view
from which we come at last to regard the world. The
lives that you admire, the attitudes that seem noble
to you are not the result of training at home, by a
father, or by masters at school, they have sprung from
beginnings of a very different order, by reaction from
the influence of everything evil or commonplace that

prevailed round about them. They represent a struggle and a victory. I can see that the picture of what we once were, in early youth, may not be recognizable and cannot, certainly, be pleasing to contemplate in later life. But we must not deny the truth of it, for it is evidence that we have really lived, that it is in accordance with the laws of life and of the mind that we have, from the common elements of life, of the life of studios, of artistic groups—assuming that one is a painter—extracted something that goes beyond them."

The Four Loves

C.S. Lewis

There is no safe investment. To love at all is to be vulnerable. Love anything, and your heart will certainly be wrung and possibly be broken. If you want to make sure of keeping it intact, you must give your heart to no one, not even an animal. Wrap it carefully round with hobbies and little luxuries; avoid all entanglements; lock it up safe in the casket or coffin of your selfishness. But in that casket — safe, dark, motionless, airless — it will change. It will not be broken; it will become unbreakable, impenetrable, irredeemable. The alternative to tragedy, or at least to the risk of tragedy, is damnation. The only place outside Heaven where you can be perfectly safe from all the dangers and perturbations of love is Hell. I believe that the most lawless and inordinate loves are less contrary to God's will than a self-invited and self-protective lovelessness...We shall draw nearer to God, not by trying to avoid the sufferings inherent in all loves, but by accepting them and offering them to Him; throwing away all defensive armor. If our hearts need to be broken, and if He chooses this as a way in which they should break, so be it. What I know about love and believe about love and giving ones heart began in this.

Napoleon Bonaparte Love Letter to Josephine Bonaparte

I have received all your letters, but none has made
me such an impression as the last. How, my beloved,
can you write to me like that? Don't you think my
position is cruel enough, without adding my sorrows
and crushing my spirit? What a style! What feelings
you show! They are fire, and they burn my poor heart.
My one and only Josephine, apart from you there is
no joy; away from you, the world is a desert where I
am alone and cannot open my heart. You have taken
more than my soul; you are the one thought of my
life. When I am tired of the worry of work, when I
feel the outcome, when men annoy me, when I am
ready to curse being alive, I put my hand on my heart;
your portrait hangs there, I look at it, and love brings
me perfect happiness, and all is miling except the
time I must spend away from my mistress.

By what art have you captivated all my facilities
and concentrated my whole being in you? It is a
sweet friend, that will die only when I do. To live for
Josephine, that is the history of my life I long. I try to
come near you. Fool! I don't notice that I am going
further away. How many countries separate us! How
long before you will read these words, this feeble
expression of a captive soul where you are queen? Oh,
my adorable wife! I don't know what fate has in store
for me, but if it keeps me apart from you any longer,
it will be unbearable! My courage is not enough for
that. Once upon a time I was proud of my courage,

and sometimes I would think of the ills destiny might bring me and consider the most terrible horrors without blinking or feeling shaken. But, today the thought that my Josephine might be in trouble, that she may be ill, above the cruel, the awful thought that she may love me less blights my soul, stills my blood and makes me sad and depressed, without even the courage of rage and despair. I used often to say men cannot harm one who dies without regret; but, now, to die not loved by you, to die without knowing, would be the torment of Hell, the living image of utter desolation. I feel I am suffocating. My one companion, you whom fate has destined to travel the sorry road of life beside me, the day I lose your heart will be the day Nature loses warmth and life for me. I stop, sweet friend; my soul is sad, my body tired, my spirit oppressed. men bore me. I ought to hate them: they take me away from my heart.

I am at Port Maurice, near Ognelia; tomorrow I reach Albenga. The two armies are moving, trying to outwit each other. Victory to the cleverer. I am pleased with Beauliu; he maneuvers well and is stronger than his predecessor. I will beat him soundly, I hope. Don't be frightened. Love me like your eyes; but that is not enough: like yourself, more than yourself, than your thoughts, your life, all of you. Forgive me, dear love, I am raving; Nature is frail when one feels deeply, when one is loved by you

Letters to his Immortal Beloved

Ludwig Van Beethoven

July 6

My angel, my everything, my very self. – only a few
words today, and in pencil (with yours) - I shall not
be certain of my rooms here until tomorrow – what
an unnecessary waste of time - why this deep grief,
where necessity speaks - can our love exist but by
sacrifices, by not demanding everything. Can you
change it, that you are not completely mine, that I am
not completely yours? Oh God, look upon beautiful
Nature and calm your mind about what must be –
love demands everything and completely with good
reason, that is how it is for me with you, and for you
with me - only you forget too easily, that I must live
for myself and for you as well, if we were wholly
united, you would not feel this as painfully, just as
little as I would – my journey was terrible. I did not
arrive here until 4 o'clock yesterday morning. As there
were few horses, the mail coach chose another route,
but what a dreadful one this was! At the last stage but
one I was warned not to travel at night; attempts were
made to frighten me about a forest, but that only
made me more eager. – I was wrong. The coach broke
down on the awful road, a road without a proper
surface, a country one. If the two coachmen had not
been with me, I would have remained stranded on the
way. Esterhazi traveled the usual road here and had
the same fate with eight horses that I had with four.

– Yet I did get some pleasure out of it, as I always do when I successfully overcome difficulties. – now quickly to the interior from the exterior. We will probably see each other soon, only, today I cannot convey to you my observations which I made during these few days about my life – If our hearts were always close together, I would have no such thoughts. my heart is full with so much to tell you - Oh - There are moments when I feel that language is nothing at all - cheer up - remain my faithful only darling, my everything, as I for you, the rest is up to the Gods, what must be for us and what is in store for us. – your faithful Ludwig

Evening, Monday, July 6

You are suffering, my dearest creature - only now have I learned that letters must be posted very early in the morning on Mondays to Thursdays - the only days on which the mail-coach goes from here to K. - You are suffering - Ah, wherever I am, there you are also - I will arrange it with you and me that I can live with you. What a life!!! thus!!! without you - pursued by the goodness of mankind hither and thither - which I as little want to deserve as I deserve it - Humility of man towards man - it pains me - and when I consider myself in relation to the universe, what am I and what is He - whom we call the greatest - and yet - herein lies the divine in man - I weep when I reflect that you will probably not receive the first report from me until Saturday - Much as you love me - I love you more - But do not ever conceal yourself from me - good night - As I am taking the baths I must go to bed - Oh God - so near! so far! Is not our love truly a heavenly structure, and also as firm as the vault of heaven.

Good morning, on July 7

Though still in bed, my thoughts go out to you, my Immortal Beloved, now and then joyfully, then sadly, waiting to learn whether or not fate will hear us - I can live only wholly with you or not at all - Yes, I am resolved to wander so long away from you until I can fly to your arms and say that I am really at home with you, and can send my soul enwrapped in you into the land of spirits - Yes, unhappily it must be so - You will be the more contained since you know my fidelity to you. No one else can ever possess my heart - never - never - Oh God, why must one be parted from one whom one so loves. And yet my life in V is now a wretched life - Your love makes me at once the happiest and the unhappiest of men - At my age I need a steady, quiet life - can that be so in our connection? My angel, I have just been told that the mailcoach goes every day - therefore I must close at once so that you may receive the letter at once - Be calm, only by a clam consideration of our existence can we achieve our purpose to live together - Be calm - love me - today - yesterday - what tearful longings for you - you - you - my life - my all - farewell. Oh continue to love me - never misjudge the most faithful heart of your beloved.
ever thine
ever mine
ever ours

Love Letter to Adele Foucher

Victor Hugo

After the two delightful evenings spent yesterday and the day before, I shall certainly not go out tonight, but will sit here at home and write to you.
Besides, my Adele, my adorable and adored Adele, what have I not to tell you?
O, God! for two days, I have been asking myself every moment if such happiness is not a dream.
It seems to me that what I feel is not of earth. I cannot yet comprehend this cloudless heaven.
You do not yet know, Adele, to what I had resigned myself. Alas, do I know it myself?
Because I was weak, I fancied I was calm; because I was preparing myself for all the mad follies of despair, I thought I was courageous and resigned.
Ah! let me cast myself humbly at your feet, you who are so grand, so tender and strong!
I had been thinking that the utmost limit of my devotion could only be the sacrifice of my life; but you, my generous love, were ready to sacrifice for me the repose of yours.
You have been privileged to receive every gift from nature, you have both fortitude and tears.
Oh, Adele, do not mistake these words for blind enthusiasm - enthusiasm for you has lasted all my life, and increased day by day.
My whole soul is yours.
If my entire existence had not been yours, the harmony of my being would have been lost, and I must have died -- died inevitably.

These were my meditations, Adele, when the letter
that was to bring me hope of else despair arrived.
If you love me, you know what must have been
my joy. What I know you may have felt, I will not
describe.
My Adele, why is there no word for this but joy? Is it
because there is no power in human speech to express
such happiness?
The sudden bound from mournful resignation to
infinite felicity seemed to upset me. Even now I am
still beside myself and sometimes I tremble lest I
should suddenly awaken from this dream divine.
Oh, now you are mine! At last you are mine! Soon --
in a few months, perhaps, my angel will sleep in my
arms, will awaken in my arms, will live there.
All your thoughts at all moments, all your looks will
be for me; all my thoughts, all my moments, all my
looks, will be for you!
 My Adele!
Adieu, my angel, my beloved Adele! Adieu!
I will kiss your hair and go to bed.
Still I am far from you, but I can dream of you.

Soon perhaps you will be at my side.
Adieu; pardon the delirium of your husband who
embraces you, and who adores you, both for this life
and another.

Letters to a Young Poet

Rainer Maria Wilke

It is also good to love: because love is difficult. For one
human being to love another human being: that is
perhaps the most difficult task that has been entrusted
to us, the ultimate task, the final test and proof, the
work for which all other work is merely preparation.
That is why young people, who are beginners in
everything, are not yet capable of love: it is something
they must learn. With their whole being, with all their
forces, gathered around their solitary, anxious, upward-
beating heart, they must learn to love. But learning-
time is always a long, secluded time, and therefore
loving, for a long time ahead and far on into life, is:
solitude, a heightened and deepened kind of aloneness
for the person who loves. Loving does not at first
mean merging, surrendering, and uniting with another
person (for what would a union be of two people who
are unclarified, unfinished, and still incoherent?), it is a
high inducement for the individual to ripen, to become
something in himself, to become world, to become
world in himself for the sake of another person; it
is a great, demanding claim on him, something that
chooses him and calls him to vast distances. Only in
this sense, as the task of working on themselves ("to
hearken and to hammer day and night"), may young
people use the love that is given to them. Merging and
surrendering and every kind of communion is not for
them (who must still, for a long, long time, save and
gather themselves); it is the ultimate, is perhaps that
for which human lives are as yet barely large enough.

Walden

Henry David Thoreau

I went to the woods because I wished to live deliberately, to front only the essential facts of life, and see if I could not learn what it had to teach, and not, when I came to die, discover that I had not lived. I did not wish to live what was not life, living is so dear; nor did I wish to practice resignation, unless it was quite necessary. I wanted to live deep and suck out all the marrow of life, to live so sturdily and Spartan-like as to put to rout all that was not life, to cut a broad swath and shave close, to drive life into a corner, and reduce it to its lowest terms, and, if it proved to be mean, why then to get the whole and genuine meanness of it, and publish its meanness to the world; or if it were sublime, to know it by experience, and be able to give a true account of it in my next excursion. For most men, it appears to me, are in a strange uncertainty about it, whether it is of the devil or of God, and have somewhat hastily concluded that it is the chief end of man here to "glorify God and enjoy him forever."

Advice to Youth

Mark Twain

Being told I would be expected to talk here, I inquired what sort of talk I ought to make. They said it should be something suitable to youth-- something didactic, instructive, or something in the nature of good advice. Very well. I have a few things in my mind which I have often longed to say for the instruction of the young; for it is in one's tender early years that such things will best take root and be most enduring and most valuable. First, then. I will say to you my young friends--and I say it beseechingly, urgingly--

Always obey your parents, when they are present. This is the best policy in the long run, because if you don't, they will make you. Most parents think they know better than you do, and you can generally make more by humoring that superstition than you can by acting on your own better judgment.

Be respectful to your superiors, if you have any, also to strangers, and sometimes to others. If a person offend you, and you are in doubt as to whether it was intentional or not, do not resort to extreme measures; simply watch your chance and hit him with a brick. That will be sufficient. If you shall find that he had not intended any offense, come out frankly and confess yourself in the wrong when you struck him; acknowledge it like a man and say you didn't mean to. Yes, always avoid violence; in this age of charity and kindliness, the time has gone by for such things. Leave dynamite to the low and unrefined.

Go to bed early, get up early--this is wise. Some authorities say get up with the sun; some say get up with one thing, others with another. But a lark is really the best thing to get up with. It gives you a splendid reputation with everybody to know that you get up with the lark; and if you get the right kind of lark, and work at him right, you can easily train him to get up at half past nine, every time--it's no trick at all.

A Wind-Storm in the Forests

John Muir

The mountain winds, like the dew and rain, sunshine and snow, are measured and bestowed with love on the forests to develop their strength and beauty. However restricted the scope of other forest influences, that of the winds is universal. The snow bends and trims the upper forests every winter, the lightning strikes a single tree here and there, while avalanches mow down thousands at a swoop as a gardener trims out a bed of flowers. But the winds go to every tree, fingering every leaf and branch and furrowed bole; not one is forgotten; the Mountain Pine towering with outstretched arms on the rugged buttresses of the icy peaks, the lowliest and most retiring tenant of the dells; they seek and find them all, caressing them tenderly, bending them in lusty exercise, stimulating their growth, plucking off a leaf or limb as required, or removing an entire tree or grove, now whispering and cooing through the branches like a sleepy child, now roaring like the ocean; the winds blessing the forests, the forests the winds, with ineffable beauty and harmony as the sure result.

After one has seen pines six feet in diameter bending like grasses before a mountain gale, and ever and anon some giant falling with a crash that shakes the hills, it seems astonishing that any, save the lowest thickset trees, could ever have found a period sufficiently stormless to establish themselves; or, once established, that they should not, sooner or later, have been blown down. But when the storm is over, and we behold the same forests tranquil again, towering fresh and unscathed in erect majesty, and consider what centuries of storms have fallen upon them since they were first planted--hail, to break the tender seedlings; lightning, to scorch and shatter; snow, winds, and avalanches, to crush and overwhelm--while the manifest result of all this wild storm-culture is the glorious perfection we behold; then faith in Nature's forestry is established, and we cease to deplore the violence of her most destructive gales, or of any other storm-implement whatsoever.

Because I Could Not Stop for Death

Emily Dickinson

Because I could not stop for Death,
He kindly stopped for me;
The carriage held but just ourselves
And Immortality.

We slowly drove, he knew no haste,
And I had put away
My labour, and my leisure too,
For his civility.

We passed the school where children played,
Their lessons scarcely done;
We passed the fields of gazing grain,
We passed the setting sun.

We paused before a house that seemed
A swelling of the ground;
The roof was scarcely visible,
The cornice but a mound.

Since then 'tis centuries; but each
Feels shorter than the day
I first surmised the horses' heads
Were toward eternity.

O Captain! My Captain!

Walt Whitman

O CAPTAIN! my Captain, our fearful trip is done,
The ship has weather'd every rack, the prize we
sought is won, The port is near, the bells I hear, the
people all exulting, While follow eyes the steady keel,
the vessel grim and daring; But O heart! heart! heart!
O the bleeding drops of red, Where on the deck my
Captain lies, Fallen cold and dead.

O Captain! my Captain! rise up and hear the bells;
Rise up--for you the flag is flung--for you the bugle
trills, For you bouquets and ribbon'd wreaths--for you
the shores a-crowding, For you they call, the swaying
mass, their eager faces turning; Here Captain! dear
father! The arm beneath your head! It is some dream
that on the deck, You've fallen cold and dead.

My Captain does not answer, his lips are pale and
still, My father does not feel my arm, he has no pulse
nor will, The ship is anchor'd safe and sound, its
voyage closed and done, From fearful trip the victor
ship comes in with object won; Exult O shores and
ring O bells! But I with mournful tread, Walk the
deck my Captain lies, Fallen Cold and Dead.

Les Miserables

Victor Hugo

What did he do during this journey? Of what was he
thinking? As in the morning, he watched the trees,
the thatched roofs, the tilled fields pass by, and the
way in which the landscape, broken at every turn of
the road, vanished; this is a sort of contemplation
which sometimes suffices to the soul, and almost
relieves it from thought. What is more melancholy
and more profound than to see a thousand objects for
the first and the last time? To travel is to be born and
to die at every instant; perhaps, in the vaguest region
of his mind, he did make comparisons between the
shifting horizon and our human existence: all the
things of life are perpetually fleeing before us; the
dark and bright intervals are intermingled; after a
dazzling moment, an eclipse; we look, we hasten, we
stretch out our hands to grasp what is passing; each
event is a turn in the road, and, all at once, we are old;
we feel a shock; all is black; we distinguish an obscure
door; the gloomy horse of life, which has been
drawing us halts, and we see a veiled and unknown
person unharnessing amid the shadows.

The Road Not Taken

Robert Frost

Two roads diverged in a yellow wood,
And sorry I could not travel both
And be one traveler, long I stood
And looked down one as far as I could
To where it bent in the undergrowth;

Then took the other, as just as fair,
And having perhaps the better claim,
Because it was grassy and wanted wear;
Though as for that the passing there
Had worn them really about the same,

And both that morning equally lay
In leaves no step had trodden black.
Oh, I kept the first for another day!
Yet knowing how way leads on to way,
I doubted if I should ever come back.

I shall be telling this with a sigh
Somewhere ages and ages hence:
Two roads diverged in a wood, and I—
I took the one less travelled by,
And that has made all the difference.

Composed upon Westminster Bridge

William Wordsworth

Earth has not anything to show more fair:
Dull would he be of soul who could pass by
A sight so touching in its majesty:
This City now doth, like a garment, wear
The beauty of the morning; silent, bare,
Ships, towers, domes, theatres and temples lie
Open unto the fields, and to the sky;
All bright and glittering in the smokeless air.
Never did sun more beautifully steep
In his first splendour, valley, rock, or hill;
Ne'er saw I, never felt, a calm so deep!
The river glideth at his own sweet will:
Dear God! The very houses seem asleep;
And all that mighty heart is lying still!

The New Colossus

Emma Lazarus

Not like the brazen giant of Greek fame,
With conquering limbs astride from land to land;
Here at our sea-washed, sunset gates shall stand
A mighty woman with a torch, whose flame
Is the imprisoned lightning, and her name
Mother of Exiles. From her beacon-hand
Glows world-wide welcome; her mild eyes command
The air-bridged harbor that twin cities frame.
"Keep, ancient lands, your storied pomp!" cries she
With silent lips. "Give me your tired, your poor,
Your huddled masses yearning to breathe free,
The wretched refuse of your teeming shore.
Send these, the homeless, tempest-tost to me,
I lift my lamp beside the golden door!"

Snow-Flakes

Henry Wadsworth Longfellow

Out of the bosom of the Air,
Out of the cloud-folds of her garments shaken,
Over the woodlands brown and bare,
Over the harvest-fields forsaken,
Silent, and soft, and slow
Descends the snow.

Even as our cloudy fancies take
Suddenly shape in some divine expression,
Even as the troubled heart doth make
In the white countenance confession,
The troubled sky reveals
The grief it feels.

This is the poem of the air,
Slowly in silent syllables recorded;
This is the secret of despair,
Long in its cloudy bosom hoarded,
Now whispered and revealed
To wood and field.

Jeanie With The Light Brown Hair

Stephen Foster

I dream of Jeanie with the light brown hair,
Borne, like a vapor, on the summer air;
I see her tripping where the bright streams play,
Happy as the daisies that dance on her way.
Many were the wild notes her merry voice would
pour,
Many were the blithe birds that warbled them o'er:
Oh! I dream of Jeanie with the light brown hair,
Floating, like a vapor, on the soft summer air.

I long for Jeanie with the daydawn smile,
Radiant in gladness, warm with winning guile;
I hear her melodies, like joys gone by,
Sighing round my heart o'er the fond hopes that die:
Sighing like the night wind and sobbing like the rain,
Wailing for the lost one that comes not again:
Oh! I long for Jeanie, and my heart bows low,
Never more to find her where the bright waters flow.

I sigh for Jeanie, but her light form strayed
Far from the fond hearts round her native glade;
Her smiles have vanished and her sweet songs flown,
Flitting like the dreams that have cheered us and
gone.
Now the nodding wild flowers may wither on the
shore
While her gentle fingers will cull them no more:
Oh! I sigh for Jeanie with the light brown hair,
Floating, like a vapor, on the soft summer air.

Treatise on the Emendation of the Intellect

Baruch Spinoza

After experience had taught me that all the things which regularly occur in ordinary life are empty and futile, and I saw that all the things which were the cause or object of my fear had nothing of good or bad in themselves, except insofar as [my] mind was moved by them, I resolved at last to try to find out whether there was anything which would be the true good, capable of communicating itself, and which alone would affect the mind, all others being rejected - whether there was something which, once found and acquired, would continuously give me the greatest joy, to eternity.

I say that "I resolved at last" for at first glance it seemed ill-advised to be willing to lose something certain for something then uncertain.

I saw, of course, the advantages that honor and wealth bring, and that I would be forced to abstain from seeking them, if I wished to devote myself to something new and different; and if by chance the greatest happiness lay in them, I saw that I would have to do without it. But if it did not lie in them, and I devoted my energies only to acquiring them, then I would equally go without it.

Ethics

Aristotle

The wise man does not expose himself needlessly
to danger, since there are few things for which he
cares sufficiently; but he is willing, in great crises,
to give even his life--knowing that under certain
conditions it is not worth while to live. He is of a
disposition to do men service, though he is ashamed
to have a service done to him. To confer a kindness
is a mark of superiority; to receive one is a mark
of subordination... He does not take part in public
displays... He is open in his dislikes and preferences;
he talks and acts frankly, because of his contempt for
men and things... He is never fired with admiration,
since there is nothing great in his eyes. He cannot
live in complaisance with others, except it be a friend;
complaisance is the characteristic of a slave... He
never feels malice, and always forgets and passes over
injuries... He is not fond of talking... It is no concern
of his that he should be praised, or that others should
be blamed. He does not speak evil of others, even of
his enemies, unless it be to themselves. His carriage is
sedate, his voice deep, his speech measured; he is not
given to hurry, for he is concerned about only a few
things; he is not prone to vehemence, for he thinks
nothing very important. A shrill voice and hasty steps
come to a man through care... He bears the accidents
of life with dignity and grace, making the best of his
circumstances, like a skillful general who marshals

his limited forces with the strategy of war... He is his own best friend, and takes delight in privacy whereas the man of no virtue or ability is his own worst enemy, and is afraid of solitude.

Pirates of Penzance

W.S. Gilbert (Gilbert and Sullivan)

I am the very model of a modern Major-General,
I've information vegetable, animal, and mineral,
I know the kings of England, and I quote the fights
historical
From Marathon to Waterloo, in order categorical;
I'm very well acquainted, too, with matters
mathematical,
I understand equations, both the simple and
quadratical,
About binomial theorem I'm teeming with a lot o'
news,
With many cheerful facts about the square of the
hypotenuse.

I'm very good at integral and differential calculus;
I know the scientific names of beings animalculous:
In short, in matters vegetable, animal, and mineral,
I am the very model of a modern Major-General.

I know our mythic history, King Arthur's and Sir
Caradoc's;
I answer hard acrostics, I've a pretty taste for paradox,
I quote in elegiacs all the crimes of Heliogabalus,
In conics I can floor peculiarities parabolous;
I can tell undoubted Raphaels from Gerard Dows
and Zoffanies,
I know the croaking chorus from The Frogs of
Aristophanes!
Then I can hum a fugue of which I've heard the

music's din afore,
And whistle all the airs from that infernal nonsense
Pinafore.

Then I can write a washing bill in Babylonic
cuneiform,
And tell you ev'ry detail of Caractacus's uniform:
In short, in matters vegetable, animal, and mineral,
I am the very model of a modern Major-General.

In fact, when I know what is meant by "mamelon"
and "ravelin",
When I can tell at sight a Mauser rifle from a javelin,
When such affairs as sorties and surprises I'm more
wary at,
 And when I know precisely what is meant by
"commissariat",
When I have learnt what progress has been made in
modern gunnery,
When I know more of tactics than a novice in a
nunnery—
In short, when I've a smattering of elemental
strategy—
You'll say a better Major-General has never sat a-gee.

For my military knowledge, though I'm plucky and
adventury,
Has only been brought down to the beginning of the
century;
But still, in matters vegetable, animal, and mineral,
I am the very model of a modern Major-General.

The Cremation of Sam McGee

Robert Service

There are strange things done in the midnight sun
By the men who moil for gold;
The Arctic trails have their secret tales
That would make your blood run cold;
The Northern Lights have seen queer sights,
But the queerest they ever did see
Was that night on the marge of Lake Lebarge
I cremated Sam McGee.

Now Sam McGee was from Tennessee, where the
cotton blooms and blows.
Why he left his home in the South to roam 'round
the Pole, God only knows.
He was always cold, but the land of gold seemed to
hold him like a spell;
Though he'd often say in his homely way that "he'd
sooner live in hell."

On a Christmas Day we were mushing our way over
the Dawson trail.
Talk of your cold! through the parka's fold it stabbed
like a driven nail.
If our eyes we'd close, then the lashes froze till
sometimes we couldn't see;
It wasn't much fun, but the only one to whimper was
Sam McGee.

And that very night, as we lay packed tight in our
robes beneath the snow,

And the dogs were fed, and the stars o'erhead were dancing heel and toe,
He turned to me, and "Cap," says he, "I'll cash in this trip, I guess;
And if I do, I'm asking that you won't refuse my last request."

Well, he seemed so low that I couldn't say no; then he says with a sort of moan:
"It's the cursèd cold, and it's got right hold, till I'm chilled clean through to the bone.
Yet 'tain't being dead — it's my awful dread of the icy grave that pains;
So I want you to swear that, foul or fair, you'll cremate my last remains."

A pal's last need is a thing to heed, so I swore I would not fail;
And we started on at the streak of dawn; but God! he looked ghastly pale.
He crouched on the sleigh, and he raved all day of his home in Tennessee;
And before nightfall a corpse was all that was left of Sam McGee.

There wasn't a breath in that land of death, and I hurried, horror-driven,
With a corpse half hid that I couldn't get rid, because of a promise given;
It was lashed to the sleigh, and it seemed to say: "You may tax your brawn and brains,
But you promised true, and it's up to you, to cremate those last remains."

Now a promise made is a debt unpaid, and the trail
has its own stern code.
In the days to come, though my lips were dumb, in
my heart how I cursed that load.
In the long, long night, by the lone firelight, while the
huskies, round in a ring,
Howled out their woes to the homeless snows — Oh
God! how I loathed the thing.

And every day that quiet clay seemed to heavy and
heavier grow;
And on I went, though the dogs were spent and the
grub was getting low;
The trail was bad, and I felt half mad, but I swore I
would not give in;
And I'd often sing to the hateful thing, and it
hearkened with a grin.

Till I came to the marge of Lake Lebarge, and a
derelict there lay;
It was jammed in the ice, but I saw in a trice it was
called the "Alice May."
And I looked at it, and I thought a bit, and I looked
at my frozen chum;
Then "Here," said I, with a sudden cry, "is my cre-ma-
tor-eum."

Some planks I tore from the cabin floor, and I lit the
boiler fire;
Some coal I found that was lying around, and I
heaped the fuel higher;
The flames just soared, and the furnace roared — such
a blaze you seldom see;

And I burrowed a hole in the glowing coal, and I stuffed in Sam McGee.

Then I made a hike, for I didn't like to hear him sizzle so;
And the heavens scowled, and the huskies howled, and the wind began to blow.
It was icy cold, but the hot sweat rolled down my cheeks, and I don't know why;
And the greasy smoke in an inky cloak went streaking down the sky.

I do not know how long in the snow I wrestled with grisly fear;
But the stars came out and they danced about ere again I ventured near;
I was sick with dread, but I bravely said: "I'll just take a peep inside.
I guess he's cooked, and it's time I looked"; ... then the door I opened wide.

And there sat Sam, looking cool and calm, in the heart of the furnace roar;
And he wore a smile you could see a mile, and said: "Please close that door.
It's fine in here, but I greatly fear, you'll let in the cold and storm —
Since I left Plumtree, down in Tennessee, it's the first time I've been warm."

There are strange things done in the midnight sun
By the men who moil for gold;
The Arctic trails have their secret tales

That would make your blood run cold;
The Northern Lights have seen queer sights,
But the queerest they ever did see
Was that night on the marge of Lake Lebarge
I cremated Sam McGee.

Hamlet

William Shakespeare

To be, or not to be, that is the question:
Whether 'tis Nobler in the mind to suffer
The Slings and Arrows of outrageous Fortune,
Or to take Arms against a Sea of troubles,
And by opposing end them: to die, to sleep
No more; and by a sleep, to say we end
The heart-ache, and the thousand Natural shocks
That Flesh is heir to? 'Tis a consummation
Devoutly to be wished. To die to sleep,
To sleep, perchance to Dream; Ay, there's the rub,
For in that sleep of death, what dreams may come,
When we have shuffled off this mortal coil,
Must give us pause. There's the respect
That makes Calamity of so long life:
For who would bear the Whips and Scorns of time,
The Oppressor's wrong, the proud man's Contumely,
[poor]
The pangs of despised Love, the Law's delay,
[disprized]
The insolence of Office, and the Spurns
That patient merit of the unworthy takes,
When he himself might his Quietus make
With a bare Bodkin? Who would Fardels bear,
To grunt and sweat under a weary life,
But that the dread of something after death,
The undiscovered Country, from whose bourn
No Traveller returns, Puzzles the will,
And makes us rather bear those ills we have,
Than fly to others that we know not of.

Thus Conscience does make Cowards of us all,
And thus the Native hue of Resolution
Is sicklied o'er, with the pale cast of Thought,
And enterprises of great pitch and moment, [pith]
With this regard their Currents turn awry, [away]
And lose the name of Action. Soft you now,
The fair Ophelia? Nymph, in thy Orisons
Be all my sins remembered.

Annabel Lee

Edgar Allan Poe

It was many and many a year ago,
In a kingdom by the sea,
That a maiden there lived whom you may know
By the name of Annabel Lee;
And this maiden she lived with no other thought
Than to love and be loved by me.

I was a child and she was a child,
In this kingdom by the sea;
But we loved with a love that was more than love-
I and my Annabel Lee;
With a love that the winged seraphs of heaven
Coveted her and me.

And this was the reason that, long ago,
In this kingdom by the sea,
A wind blew out of a cloud, chilling
My beautiful Annabel Lee;
So that her highborn kinsman came
And bore her away from me,
To shut her up in a sepulchre
In this kingdom by the sea.

The angels, not half so happy in heaven,
Went envying her and me-
Yes!- that was the reason (as all men know,
In this kingdom by the sea)
That the wind came out of the cloud by night,
Chilling and killing my Annabel Lee.

But our love it was stronger by far than the love
Of those who were older than we-
Of many far wiser than we-
And neither the angels in heaven above,
Nor the demons down under the sea,
Can ever dissever my soul from the soul
Of the beautiful Annabel Lee.

For the moon never beams without bringing me
dreams
Of the beautiful Annabel Lee;
And the stars never rise but I feel the bright eyes
Of the beautiful Annabel Lee;
And so, all the night-tide, I lie down by the side
Of my darling- my darling- my life and my bride,
In the sepulchre there by the sea,
In her tomb by the sounding sea.

Gus the Theatre Cat

T.S. Elliot

Gus is the Cat at the Theatre Door.
His name, as I ought to have told you before,
Is really Asparagus. That's such a fuss
To pronounce, that we usually call him just Gus.
His coat's very shabby, he's thin as a rake,
And he suffers from palsy that makes his paw shake.
Yet he was, in his youth, quite the smartest of Cats--
But no longer a terror to mice and to rats.
For he isn't the Cat that he was in his prime;
Though his name was quite famous, he says, in its
time.
And whenever he joins his friends at their club
(Which takes place at the back of the neighbouring
pub)
He loves to regale them, if someone else pays,
With anecdotes drawn from his palmiest days.
For he once was a Star of the highest degree--
He has acted with Irving, he's acted with Tree.
And he likes to relate his success on the Halls,
Where the Gallery once gave him seven cat-calls.
But his grandest creation, as he loves to tell,
Was Firefrorefiddle, the Fiend of the Fell.

"I have played," so he says, "every possible part,
And I used to know seventy speeches by heart.
I'd extemporize back-chat, I knew how to gag,
And I knew how to let the cat out of the bag.
I knew how to act with my back and my tail;
With an hour of rehearsal, I never could fail.

I'd a voice that would soften the hardest of hearts,
Whether I took the lead, or in character parts.
I have sat by the bedside of poor Little Nell;
When the Curfew was rung, then I swung on the
bell.
In the Pantomime season I never fell flat,
And I once understudied Dick Whittington's Cat.
But my grandest creation, as history will tell,
Was Firefrorefiddle, the Fiend of the Fell."

Then, if someone will give him a toothful of gin,
He will tell how he once played a part in East Lynne.
At a Shakespeare performance he once walked on pat,
When some actor suggested the need for a cat.
He once played a Tiger--could do it again--
Which an Indian Colonel purused down a drain.
And he thinks that he still can, much better than
most,
Produce blood-curdling noises to bring on the Ghost.
And he once crossed the stage on a telegraph wire,
To rescue a child when a house was on fire.
And he says: "Now then kittens, they do not get
trained
As we did in the days when Victoria reigned.
They never get drilled in a regular troupe,
And they think they are smart, just to jump through
a hoop."
And he'll say, as he scratches himself with his claws,
"Well, the Theatre's certainly not what it was.
These modern productions are all very well,
But there's nothing to equal, from what I hear tell,
That moment of mystery
When I made history

As Firefrorefiddle, the Fiend of the Fell."

The Song of Hiawatha

Henry Wadsworth Longfellow

By the shore of Gitchie Gumee,
By the shining Big-Sea-Water,
At the doorway of his wigwam,
In the pleasant Summer morning,
Hiawatha stood and waited.
All the air was full of freshness,
All the earth was bright and joyous,
And before him through the sunshine,
Westward toward the neighboring forest
Passed in golden swarms the Ahmo,
Passed the bees, the honey-makers,
Burning, singing in the sunshine.
Bright above him shown the heavens,
Level spread the lake before him;
From its bosom leaped the sturgeon,
Aparkling, flashing in the sunshine;
On its margin the great forest
Stood reflected in the water,
Every tree-top had its shadow,
Motionless beneath the water.
From the brow of Hiawatha
Gone was every trace of sorrow,
As the fog from off the water,
And the mist from off the meadow.
With a smile of joy and triumph,
With a look of exultation,
As of one who in a vision
Sees what is to be, but is not,
Stood and waited Hiawatha.

Charge of the Light Brigade

Alfred Lord Tennyson

Half a league, half a league,
Half a league onward,
All in the valley of Death
Rode the six hundred.
`Forward, the Light Brigade!
Charge for the guns!' he said:
Into the valley of Death
Rode the six hundred.

`Forward, the Light Brigade!'
Was there a man dismay'd?
Not tho' the soldier knew
some one had blunder'd:
Theirs not to make reply,
Theirs not to reason why,
Theirs but to do and die:
Into the valley of Death
Rode the six hundred.

Cannon to right of them,
Cannon to left of them,
Cannon in front of them
Volley'd and thunder'd;
Storm'd at with shot and shell,
Boldly they rode and well,
Into the jaws of Death,
Into the mouth of Hell
Rode the six hundred.

Flash'd all their sabres bare,
Flash'd as they turn'd in air
Sabring the gunners there,
Charging an army, while
All the world wonder'd:
Plunged in the battery-smoke
Right thro' the line they broke;
Cossack and Russian
Reel'd from the sabre-stroke
Shatter'd and sunder'd.
Then they rode back, but not
Not the six hundred.

Cannon to right of them,
Cannon to left of them,
Cannon behind them
Volley'd and thunder'd;
Storm'd at with shot and shell,
While horse and hero fell,
They that had fought so well
Came thro' the jaws of Death,
Back from the mouth of Hell,
All that was left of them,
Left of six hundred.

When can their glory fade?
O the wild charge they made!
All the world wonder'd.
Honour the charge they made!
Honour the Light Brigade,
Noble six hundred!

Beautiful Dreamer

Stephen Foster

Beautiful dreamer, wake unto me,
Starlight and dewdrops are waiting for thee;
Sounds of the rude world heard in the day,
Lull'd by the moonlight have all pass'd away!

Beautiful dreamer, queen of my song,
List while I woo thee with soft melody;
Gone are the cares of life's busy throng.

Beautiful dreamer, awake unto me!
Beautiful dreamer, awake unto me!

Beautiful dreamer, out on the sea,
Mermaids are chaunting the wild lorelie;
Over the streamlet vapors are borne,
Waiting to fade at the bright coming morn.

Beautiful dreamer, beam on my heart,
E'en as the morn on the streamlet and sea;
Then will all clouds of sorrow depart,

Beautiful dreamer, awake unto me!

Main Street

Joyce Kilmer

I like to look at the blossomy track of the moon upon
the sea,
But it isn't half so fine a sight as Main Street used to
be
When it all was covered over with a couple of feet of
snow,
And over the crisp and radiant road the ringing
sleighs would go.

Now, Main Street bordered with autumn leaves, it
was a pleasant thing,
And its gutters were gay with dandelions early in the
Spring;
I like to think of it white with frost or dusty in the
heat,
Because I think it is humaner than any other street.

A city street that is busy and wide is ground by a
thousand wheels,
And a burden of traffic on its breast is all it ever feels:
It is dully conscious of weight and speed and of work
that never ends,
But it cannot be human like Main Street, and
recognise its friends.

There were only about a hundred teams on Main
Street in a day,
And twenty or thirty people, I guess, and some
children out to play.

And there wasn't a wagon or buggy, or a man or a girl
or a boy
That Main Street didn't remember, and somehow
seem to enjoy.

The truck and the motor and trolley car and the
elevated train
They make the weary city street reverberate with pain:
But there is yet an echo left deep down within my
heart
Of the music the Main Street cobblestones made
beneath a butcher's cart.

God be thanked for the Milky Way that runs across
the sky,
That's the path that my feet would tread whenever I
have to die.
Some folks call it a Silver Sword, and some a Pearly
Crown,
But the only thing I think it is, is Main Street,
Heaventown.

Stopping by Woods on a Snowy Evening

Robert Frost

Whose woods these are I think I know.
His house is in the village though;
He will not see me stopping here
To watch his woods fill up with snow.

My little horse must think it queer
To stop without a farmhouse near
Between the woods and frozen lake
The darkest evening of the year.

He gives his harness bells a shake
To ask if there is some mistake.
The only other sound's the sweep
Of easy wind and downy flake.

The woods are lovely, dark, and deep.
But I have promises to keep,
And miles to go before I sleep,
And miles to go before I sleep

Frankenstein

Mary Shelley

I expected this reception. All men hate the wretched.
How, then, must I be hated, who am miserable
beyond all living things! Yet you, my creator, detest
and spurn me, thy creature, to whom thou art bound
by ties only dissoluble by the annihilation of one of
us. You purpose to kill me. How dare you sport thus
with life? Do your duty toward me, and I will do
mine toward you and the rest of mankind. If you will
comply with my conditions, I will leave them and
you at peace, but if you refuse I will glut the maw
of death, until it be satiated with the blood of your
remaining friends. Have I not suffered enough that
you seek to increase my misery? Life, although it may
only be an accumulation of anguish, is dear to me,
and I will defend it. Remember, thou hast made me
more powerful than thyself. My height is superior
to thine, my joints more supple. But I will not be
tempted to set myself in opposition to thee. I am thy
creature and I will be even mild and docile to my
natural lord and king, if thou wilt also perform thy
part, the which thou owest me. Oh, Frankenstein, be
not equitable to every other and trample upon me
alone, to whom thy justice, and even thy clemency
and affection, is most due. Remember that I am thy
creature, I ought to by thy Adam, but I am rather
the fallen angel whom thou drivest from joy for no
misdeed. Everywhere I see bliss from which I alone
am irrevocably excluded. The desert mountains and
dreary glaciers are my refuge. I have wandered here

many days. The caves of ice, which I only do not fear, are a dwelling to me, and the only one which man does not grudge. These bleak skies I hail, for they are kinder to me than your fellow beings. If the multitude of mankind knew of my existence, they would do as you do and arm themselves for my destruction. Shall I not then hate them who abhor me? I will keep no terms with my enemies. I am miserable and they shall share my wretchedness. Yet it is in your power to recompense me, and deliver them from an evil which it only remains for you to make so great that not only you and your family, but thousands of others, shall be swallowed up in the whirlwinds of its rage. Let your compassion be moved and do not disdain me. I was benevolent and good. Misery made me a fiend. Make me happy and I shall again be virtuous. I have wandered through these mountains, I have ranged through their immense recesses, consumed by a burning passion which you alone can gratify. We may not part until you have promised to comply with my request. I am alone and miserable. Man will not associate with me, but one as deformed and horrible as myself would not deny herself to me. My companion must be of the same species and have the same defects. A female. This being you must create.

Madame Bovary

Gustave Flaubert

Deep down in her heart, she was waiting and waiting for something to happen. Like a shipwrecked mariner, she gazed out wistfully over the wide solitude of her life, if so be she might catch the white gleam of a sail away on the dim horizon. She knew not what it would be, this longed-for barque; what wind would waft it to her, or to what shores it would bear her away. She knew not if it would be a shallop or a three-decker, burdened with anguish or freighted with joy. But every morning when she awoke she hoped it would come that day. She listened to every sound, started swiftly from her bed, and could not understand why nothing happened. And then at sunset, more sad at heart than ever, she would long for the morrow to come.

"Citizenship in a Republic" Speech

Theodore Roosevelt

It is not the critic who counts: not the man who points out how the strong man stumbles or where the doer of deeds could have done better. The credit belongs to the man who is actually in the arena, whose face is marred by dust and sweat and blood, who strives valiantly, who errs and comes up short again and again, because there is no effort without error or shortcoming, but who knows the great enthusiasms, the great devotions, who spends himself for a worthy cause; who, at the best, knows, in the end, the triumph of high achievement, and who, at the worst, if he fails, at least he fails while daring greatly, so that his place shall never be with those cold and timid souls who knew neither victory nor defeat.

Auguries of Innocence

William Blake

To see a World in a Grain of Sand
And a Heaven in a Wild Flower,
Hold Infinity in the palm of your hand
And Eternity in an hour.
A Robin Red breast in a Cage
Puts all heaven in a Rage.
A dove house fill'd with doves and Pigeons
Shudders Hell thro' all its regions.
A dog starv'd at his Master's Gate
Predicts the ruin of the State.
A Horse misus'd upon the Road
Calls to Heaven for Human blood.
Each outcry of the hunted Hare
A fibre from the Brain does tear.
A Skylark wounded in the wing,
A Cherubim does cease to sing.
The Game Cock clip'd and arm'd for fight
Does the Rising Sun affright.
Every Wolf's and Lion's howl
Raises from Hell a Human Soul.
The wild deer, wand'ring here and there,
Keeps the Human Soul from Care.
The Lamb misus'd breeds Public strife
And yet forgives the Butcher's Knife.
The Bat that flits at close of Eve
Has left the Brain that won't Believe.
The Owl that calls upon the Night
Speaks the Unbeliever's fright.
He who shall hurt the little Wren

Shall never be belov'd by Men.
He who the Ox to wrath has mov'd
Shall never be by Woman lov'd.
The wanton Boy that kills the Fly
Shall feel the Spider's enmity.
He who torments the Chafer's sprite
Weaves a Bower in endless Night.
The Catterpiller on the Leaf
Repeats to thee thy Mother's grief.
Kill not the Moth nor Butterfly,
For the Last Judgement draweth nigh.
He who shall train the Horse to War
Shall never pass the Polar Bar.
The Beggar's Dog and Widow's Cat,
Feed them and thou wilt grow fat.
The Gnat that sings his Summer's song
Poison gets from Slander's tongue.
The poison of the Snake and Newt
Is the sweat of Envy's Foot.
The Poison of the Honey Bee
Is the Artist's Jealousy.
The Prince's Robes and Beggar's Rags
Are Toadstools on the Miser's Bags.
A truth that's told with bad intent.
Beats all the Lies you can invent.
It is right it should be so;
Man was made for Joy and Woe;
And when this we rightly know
Thro' the World we safely go.
Joy and Woe are woven fine,
A Clothing for the Soul divine;
Under every grief and pine
Runs a joy with silken twine.

The Babe is more than swaddling Bands;
Throughout all these Human Lands
Tools were made, and Born were hands,
Every Farmer Understands.
Every Tear from Every Eye
Becomes a Babe in Eternity;
This is caught by Females bright
And return'd to its own delight.
The Bleat, the Bark, Bellow and Roar
Are Waves that Beat on Heaven's Shore.
The Babe that weeps the Rod beneath
Writes Revenge in realms of death.
The Beggar's Rags, fluttering in Air,
Does to Rags the Heavens tear.
The Soldier, arm'd, with Sword and Gun,
Palsied strikes the Summer's Sun.
The poor Man's Farthing is worth more
Than all the Gold on Afric's Shore.
One Mite wrung from the Labrer's hands
Shall buy and sell the Miser's Lands:
Or, if protected from on high,
Does that whole Nation sell and buy.
He who mocks the Infant's Faith
Shall be mock'd in Age and Death.
He who shall teach the Child to Doubt
The rotting Grave shall ne'er get out.
He who respects the Infant's faith
Triumphs over Hell and Death.
The Child's Toys and the Old Man's Reasons
Are the Fruits of the Two seasons.
The Questioner, who sits so sly,
Shall never know how to Reply.
He who replies to words of Doubt

Doth put the Light of Knowledge out.
The Strongest Poison ever known
Came from Caesar's Laurel Crown.
Nought can deform the Human Race
Like to the Armour's iron brace.
When Gold and Gems adorn the Plow
To peaceful Arts shall Envy Bow.
A Riddle or the Cricket's Cry
Is to Doubt a fit Reply.
The Emmet's Inch and Eagle's Mile
Make Lame Philosophy to smile.
He who Doubts from what he sees
Will ne'er Believe, do what you Please.
If the Sun and Moon should doubt,
They'd immediately Go out.
To be in a Passion you Good may do,
But no Good if a Passion is in you.
The Whore and Gambler, by the State
Licenc'd, build that Nation's Fate.
The Harlot's cry from Street to Street
Shall weave Old England's winding Sheet.
The Winner's Shout, the Loser's Curse,
Dance before dead England's Hearse.
Every Night and every Morn
Some to Misery are Born.
Every Morn and every Night
Some are Born to sweet delight.
Some are Born to sweet delight,
Some are Born to Endless Night.
We are led to Believe a Lie
When we see not Thro' the Eye,
Which was Born in a Night to perish in a Night
When the Soul Slept in Beams of Light.

God Appears and God is Light
To those poor Souls who dwell in Night,
But does a Human Form Display
To those who Dwell in Realms of day

The Odyssey

Homer

On the other part are two rocks, whereof the one reaches with sharp peak to the wide heaven, and a dark cloud encompasses it; this never streams away, and there is no clear air about the peak neither in summer nor in harvest tide. No mortal man may scale it or set foot thereon, not though he had twenty hands and feet. For the rock is smooth, and sheer, as it were polished. And in the midst of the cliff is a dim cave turned to Erebus, towards the place of darkness, whereby ye shall even steer your hollow ship, noble Odysseus. Not with an arrow from a bow might a man in his strength reach from his hollow ship into that deep cave. And therein dwelleth Scylla, yelping terribly. Her voice indeed is no greater than the voice of a new-born whelp, but a dreadful monster is she, nor would any look on her gladly, not if it were a god that met her. Verily she hath twelve feet all dangling down; and six necks exceeding long, and on each a hideous head, and therein three rows of teeth set thick and close, full of black death. Up to her middle is she sunk far down in the hollow cave, but forth she holds her heads from the dreadful gulf, and there she fishes, swooping round the rock, for dolphins or sea-dogs, or whatso greater beast she may anywhere take, whereof the deep-voiced Amphitrite feeds countless flocks. Thereby no sailors boast that they have fled scatheless ever with their ship, for with each head she carries off a man, whom she hath snatched from out the dark-prowed ship.

The Walrus and the Carpenter

Lewis Carroll

The sun was shining on the sea,
Shining with all his might:
He did his very best to make
The billows smooth and bright--
And this was odd, because it was
The middle of the night.

The moon was shining sulkily,
Because she thought the sun
Had got no business to be there
After the day was done--
"It's very rude of him," she said,
"To come and spoil the fun!"

The sea was wet as wet could be,
The sands were dry as dry.
You could not see a cloud, because
No cloud was in the sky:
No birds were flying overhead--
There were no birds to fly.

The Walrus and the Carpenter
Were walking close at hand;
They wept like anything to see
Such quantities of sand:
"If this were only cleared away,"
They said, "it would be grand!"

"If seven maids with seven mops
Swept it for half a year.
Do you suppose," the Walrus said,
"That they could get it clear?"
"I doubt it," said the Carpenter,
And shed a bitter tear.

"O Oysters, come and walk with us!"
The Walrus did beseech.
"A pleasant walk, a pleasant talk,
Along the briny beach:
We cannot do with more than four,
To give a hand to each."

The eldest Oyster looked at him,
But never a word he said:
The eldest Oyster winked his eye,
And shook his heavy head--
Meaning to say he did not choose
To leave the oyster-bed.

But four young Oysters hurried up,
All eager for the treat:
Their coats were brushed, their faces washed,
Their shoes were clean and neat--
And this was odd, because, you know,
They hadn't any feet.

Four other Oysters followed them,
And yet another four;
And thick and fast they came at last,
And more, and more, and more--
All hopping through the frothy waves,
And scrambling to the shore.

The Walrus and the Carpenter
Walked on a mile or so,
And then they rested on a rock
Conveniently low:
And all the little Oysters stood
And waited in a row.

"The time has come," the Walrus said,
"To talk of many things:
Of shoes--and ships--and sealing-wax--
Of cabbages--and kings--
And why the sea is boiling hot--
And whether pigs have wings."

"But wait a bit," the Oysters cried,
"Before we have our chat;
For some of us are out of breath,
And all of us are fat!"
"No hurry!" said the Carpenter.
They thanked him much for that.

"A loaf of bread," the Walrus said,
"Is what we chiefly need:
Pepper and vinegar besides
Are very good indeed--
Now if you're ready, Oysters dear,
We can begin to feed."

"But not on us!" the Oysters cried,
Turning a little blue.
"After such kindness, that would be
A dismal thing to do!"
"The night is fine," the Walrus said.
"Do you admire the view?

"It was so kind of you to come!
And you are very nice!"
The Carpenter said nothing but
"Cut us another slice:
I wish you were not quite so deaf--
I've had to ask you twice!"

"It seems a shame," the Walrus said,
"To play them such a trick,
After we've brought them out so far,
And made them trot so quick!"
The Carpenter said nothing but
"The butter's spread too thick!"

"I weep for you," the Walrus said:
"I deeply sympathize."
With sobs and tears he sorted out
Those of the largest size,
Holding his pocket-handkerchief
Before his streaming eyes.

"O Oysters," said the Carpenter,
"You've had a pleasant run!
Shall we be trotting home again?'
But answer came there none--
And this was scarcely odd, because
They'd eaten every one.

Neither Out Far Nor In Deep

Robert Frost

The people along the sand
All turn and look one way.
They turn their back on the land.
They look at the sea all day.

As long as it takes to pass
A ship keeps raising its hull;
The wetter ground like glass
Reflects a standing gull.

The land may vary more;
But wherever the truth may be—
The water comes ashore,
And the people look at the sea.

They cannot look out far.
They cannot look in deep.
But when was that ever a bar
To any watch they keep?

From summation to the Jury – Lawsuit over killing of a dog

George Graham Vest

Gentlemen of the Jury

The one absolutely unselfish friend that man can have in this selfish world, the one that never deserts him, the one that never proves ungrateful or treacherous is his dog. A man's dog stands by him in prosperity and in poverty, in health and in sickness. He will sleep on the cold ground, where the wintry winds blow and the snow drives fiercely, if only he may be near his master's side. He will kiss the hand that has no food to offer. He will lick the wounds and sores that come in encounters with the roughness of the world. He guards the sleep of his pauper master as if he were a prince. When all other friends desert, he remains. When riches take wings, and reputation falls to pieces, he is as constant in his love as the sun in its journey through the heavens.

If fortune drives the master forth, an outcast in the world, friendless and homeless, the faithful dog asks no higher privilege than that of accompanying him, to guard him against danger, to fight against his enemies. And when the last scene of all comes, and death takes his master in its embrace and his body is laid away in the cold ground, no matter if all other friends pursue their way, there by the graveside will the noble dog be found, his head between his paws, his eyes sad, but open in alert watchfulness, faithful and true even in death.

Casey at the Bat

Ernest Lawrence Thayer

The outlook wasn't brilliant for the Mudville nine
that day;
The score stood four to two with but one inning more
to play.
And then when Cooney died at first, and Barrows did
the same,
A sickly silence fell upon of the patrons of the game.

A straggling few got up to go in deep despair. The rest
Clung to that hope which springs eternal in the
human breast.
They thought if only Casey could but get a whack at
that-
We'd put even money now with Casey at the bat.

But Flynn preceded Casey, as did also Jimmy Blake,
And the former was lulu and the latter was a cake;
So upon that stricken multitude grim melancholy sat,
For there seemed but little chance of Casey's getting
to the bat.

But Flynn let drive a single, to the wonderment of all,
And Blake, the much despised, tore the cover off the
ball;
And when the dust had lifted, and the men saw what
had occurred,
There was Johnnie safe at second, and Flynn
a-hugging third.

Then from 5,000 throats and more there rose a lusty yell;
It rumbled through the valley, it rattled in the dell;
It knocked upon the mountain and recoiled upon the flat,
For Casey, mighty Casey, was advancing to the bat.

There was ease in Casey's manner as he stepped into his place;
There was pride in Casey's bearing and a smile on Casey's face.
And when, responding to the cheers, he lightly doffed his hat,
No stranger in the crowd could doubt 'twas Casey at the bat.

Ten thousand eyes were on him as he rubbed his hands with dirt;
Five thousand tongues applauded when he wiped them on his shirt.
Then while the writhing pitcher ground the ball into his hip,
Defiance gleamed in Casey's eye, a sneer curled Casey's lip.

And now the leather-covered sphere came hurtling through the air,
And Casey stood a-watching it in haughty grandeur there.
Close by the sturdy batsman the ball unheeded sped-
"That ain't my style," said Casey. "Strike one," the umpire said.

From the benches, black with people, there went up a muffled roar,
Like the beating of the storm-waves on the stern and distant shore.
"Kill him! Kill the umpire!" shouted some one on the stand;
And it's likely they'd have killed him had not Casey raised his hand.

With a smile of Christian charity great Casey's visage shone;
He stilled the rising tumult, he bade the game go on;
He signaled to the pitcher, and once more the spheroid flew;
But Casey still ignored it, and the umpire said, "Strike Two."

"Fraud!" cried the maddened thousands, and echo answered "fraud";
But one scornful look from Casey and the audience was awed;
They saw his face grow stern and cold, they saw his muscles strain,
And they knew that Casey wouldn't let that ball go by again.

The sneer is gone from Casey's lip, his teeth are clenched in hate;
He pounds with cruel violence his bat upon the plate.
And now the pitcher holds the ball, and now he lets it go,
And now the air is shattered by the force of Casey's blow.

Oh, somewhere in this favored land the sun is shining
bright;
The band is playing somewhere, and somewhere
hearts are light,
And somewhere men are laughing, and somewhere
children shout;
But there is no joy in Mudville -mighty Casey has
struck out.